# I Desire Justice

# I Desire Justice

## Daily Reflections from Ash Wednesday to Easter Day

The students and staff of

Ridley Hall CAMBRIDGE

CANTERBURY
PRESS
Norwich

© Ridley Hall 2005

First published in 2005 by the Canterbury Press Norwich
(a publishing imprint of Hymns Ancient & Modern Limited,
a registered charity)
9–17 St Alban's Place,
London N1 0NX

www.scm-canterburypress.co.uk

Except where indicated, scripture quotations are from the
New Revised Standard Version of the Bible, copyright 1989
by the Division of Christian Education of the National
Council of the Churches of Christ in the USA. Used by
permission. All rights reserved.

British Library Cataloguing in Publication data

A catalogue record for this book is available
from the British Library

ISBN 1-85311-697-1
978-1-85311-697-1

Typeset by Regent Typesetting, London
Printed in Great Britain by
Bookmarque, Croydon, Surrey

# Contents

## What readers said about last year's Lent book

I would like to thank you once again for giving us fresh and vibrant Lenten reflections.

*J. K., Ware*

I meant to write after last year's Lent reflections: where did time go? Once again I am enjoying your Lent edition. Thank you for such an enjoyable book, I really look forward to my 10 minutes or so every night and wish to convey my thanks to all who compiled it.

*M. M., Knowle*

Again this year members of this church are using the Ridley Hall Lent book as an aid to our devotions. We have found it to be a simple but effective help to Lenten observance. Please pass on the appreciation of this parish to your students.

*J. S., Harpenden*

I have used your book daily during Lent and have found it most helpful. It is both easy to understand and very thought provoking.

*M. G., Newcastle-on-Tyne*

# Preface

## The Ridley Hall Lent Books

These Lent meditations are almost entirely the work of students training for some form of Christian ministry. Occasionally a contribution from a member of the teaching or administrative staff may also be found but, as with other reflections, not specifically identified. This is the fifth such annual publication and, apart from the first, which was very much an experiment, previous titles have each sold several thousand copies. These have had markedly different themes, all suitable for both group and individual Bible reading through Lent, as can be seen from the titles of this book's predecessors:

*We Want to See Jesus*
*We Want to Know Christ*
*The Shame and the Glory*
*His Story, Our Story*

The idea of producing an annual Lent book was conceived in prayer. A student, recognizing that the College has a constant need for financial support if it is to grow and improve its facilities, felt concerned that trainee clergy (the majority of Ridley students) could seldom give such support. He took the issue to prayer. The feeling grew strongly in him that the practice of writing short meditative pieces

based on Bible texts had to be within the grasp of the whole
community of Ridley Hall and could be the basis for the
students' support for the life of their college.

The first book was drawn together and published in
five short weeks. It generated enormous enthusiasm for
repeating the exercise in following years – and circula-
tion has climbed consistently. Each year we have felt God's
blessing on this enterprise. Letters from readers have regu-
larly expressed enthusiasm for the nature of the books and
each year people write to say how much they have been
helped by the reflections.

This year, we are delighted to be publishing the fifth Lent
book jointly with Canterbury Press. This will substantially
expand the distribution possibilities and we hope that
many new readers will come into contact with this publication, joining what has become a loyal core readership. The
daily texts and reflections can be lifted electronically from
the College website – www.ridley.cam.ac.uk – where you
will find a wealth of other information and images about
the life and work of Ridley Hall.

The timing of this book is special for the community, in
that it is produced in the 125th year of the College's life and
in the 450th year after the death of Bishop Nicholas Ridley,
who was burnt at the stake for his faith in October 1555
and after whom the College is named.

# Foreword by the Principal of Ridley Hall

It is a great delight to be able to commend the fifth Ridley Hall Lent book – especially as it is published in the 125th anniversary of the opening of the College. Our present body of one hundred and twenty men and women of varied ages and backgrounds training for ordained, youth and other ministries, is very different from the first group of eight men who came straight from their Cambridge colleges to prepare for ordination in 1881. But there is one thing that unites them – an encounter with the transformative love of God.

Like the first members of Ridley Hall, and those who followed them through the end of the nineteenth, the whole of the twentieth and the beginning of the twenty-first centuries, the people who have written these reflections have been grasped by the grace of God. They have discovered that God's love is so great that it judges anything that thwarts his purposes of love and so determined that it will go to unimaginable lengths to fulfil them. They have encountered the God of 'steadfast love', as the Old Testament likes to call him, and they have heard him say to all that binds them what he once said to Pharaoh, 'Let my people go' (Exodus 5.1). They have met the God who 'so loved the world that he gave his only Son' (John 3.16) and 'made him to be sin who knew no sin, so that in him we might become the righteousness of God' (2 Corinthians 5.21).

This God 'who is just in all his ways' (Deuteronomy 32.4), this righteous God, who desires nothing less than our transformation into embodiments of his righteousness, yearns to see his just and righteous ways lived out in our world. That is why many of those writing these Lenten reflections have given up successful and lucrative careers to step out into the dangerous territory of Christian ministry. They want the world to know the high standards of God's love. They want people to know the compassion of God for all that suffers and his rebuke to all that oppresses. They want people to turn to the God who heals and restores. They want people to be challenged and cleansed and changed by the purifying fire of God's love. They want people to hear God's timeless call to 'do justice, and to love kindness, and to walk humbly with [their] God' (Micah 6.8).

I hope that these reflections will take you *deeper* into God's saving love for the world and *further* into God's call to the world to live according to the just and righteous ways of his love.

*Christopher Cocksworth*
*November 2005*

# Using this Book

## In a group

Ridley Hall's Lent meditations have proved to be excellent 'starters' for small group discussion. The experience of many groups has been that simply talking about how the prior week's reflections have spoken to group members has been enough to generate conversations and prompt insights that have been highly valued. These have, in turn, built confidence and mutuality, sometimes to an unexpected degree. Perhaps this is because the meditations derive from the wide-ranging life experiences of Ridley's students, so easily provoke empathy and establish common ground with the readers.

## As an individual

- Each day during Lent, set aside some time in a quiet place. You will need only this book, as the relevant Bible passages accompany each reflection.
- Do whatever helps you to relax – sit somewhere quiet, make a drink, take some deep breaths.
- Pray for God's Spirit to guide you before you read; the prayer on page 1 might help.
- Read the Bible passage set for the day – slowly – and think about what it might be saying.
- Then read the reflection for the day – again slowly – and pause for thought as you go. How does it relate to the

Bible passage? Is there anything in the reflection which is similar to or different from anything you have experienced or thought before?

- When you have read and reflected, pray about what you have read and ask God what he might be saying to you through it; you might like to use the Lord's Prayer to finish.

# The Daily Reflections

*God of love,*
*you are just in all your ways.*
*By your Holy Spirit,*
*inspire us this Lent*
*to learn more of you,*
*and more of ourselves*
*that we may do justice, love kindness*
*and walk humbly with you our God,*
*through Jesus Christ our Lord.*

## Matthew 20.1–16

'For the kingdom of heaven is like a landowner who went out early in the morning to hire labourers for his vineyard. After agreeing with the labourers for the usual daily wage, he sent them into his vineyard. When he went out about nine o'clock, he saw others standing idle in the market-place; and he said to them, "You also go into the vineyard, and I will pay you whatever is right." So they went. When he went out again about noon and about three o'clock, he did the same. And about five o'clock he went out and found others standing around; and he said to them, "Why are you standing here idle all day?" They said to him, "Because no one has hired us." He said to them, "You also go into the vineyard." When evening came, the owner of the vineyard said to his manager, "Call the labourers and give them their pay, beginning with the last and then going to the first." When those hired about five o'clock came, each of them received the usual daily wage. Now when the first came, they thought they would receive more; but each of them also received the usual daily wage. And when they received it, they grumbled against the landowner, saying, "These last worked only one hour, and you have made them equal to us who have borne the burden of the day and the scorching heat." But he replied to one of them, "Friend, I am doing you no wrong; did you not agree with me for the usual daily wage? Take what belongs to you and go; I choose to give to this last the same as I give to you. Am I not allowed to do what I choose with what belongs to me? Or are you envious because I am generous?" So the last will be first, and the first will be last.'

I once spent a whole summer working for the government. Well, when I say working, I was receiving the Emergency Student Unemployment Benefit.

The thing I noticed very quickly was that working for the government wasn't much fun. I'd imagined a pretty relaxed time: lazy days on the beach with friends and long walks in the hills punctuated by occasional visits to the job centre. I wasn't ready for the feelings of uselessness, the vague suspicion that no one valued me enough to trust me with anything.

When I read this parable, my thoughts are drawn to those hired later in the day — the ones who have waited in the dusty marketplace since first light, hoping to be offered work; those who have watched while younger, fitter labourers have been snapped up on lucrative contracts; those who have spent a whole day shuffling under the sun, wondering if anyone will value them enough to trust them with anything.

The landowner in this story has work in his vineyard for everyone who wants it. And we may be surprised to learn that the day's wages do not reflect the productivity of the labourers, but the generosity of the employer. Apparently, this landowner values everyone equally.

A poor remuneration policy? More than likely. A dubious management style? Quite possibly. A picture of God's loving justice in action? Absolutely!

*Heavenly Father,*
*thank you for your word to each one of us,*
*'You also go into the vineyard.'*
*As we work for you,*
*help us to remember your gracious invitation and*
    *generosity to all.*

## Luke 6.27–36

'But I say to you that listen, Love your enemies, do good to those who hate you, bless those who curse you, pray for those who abuse you. If anyone strikes you on the cheek, offer the other also; and from anyone who takes away your coat do not withhold even your shirt. Give to everyone who begs from you; and if anyone takes away your goods, do not ask for them again. Do to others as you would have them do to you.

'If you love those who love you, what credit is that to you? For even sinners love those who love them. If you do good to those who do good to you, what credit is that to you? For even sinners do the same. If you lend to those from whom you hope to receive, what credit is that to you? Even sinners lend to sinners, to receive as much again. But love your enemies, do good, and lend, expecting nothing in return. Your reward will be great, and you will be children of the Most High; for he is kind to the ungrateful and the wicked. Be merciful, just as your Father is merciful.'

I was being stalked. Every part of my life was affected and became a covert operation. I had to move house. An injunction to keep the stalker at a distance meant that, if the stalker got to a place first, I had to leave for fear of being accused of inviting attention. I sat alone at home, isolated by the very law that sought to protect me.

Not even God's house was safe – there was the stalker when I went to church, sitting in my sanctuary pretending to be 'saved'. I began to hate.

Close friends fell away having been 'confided in'. I did not know who I was angrier with, the stalker or those who believed what was said about me.

One evening, as I prepared a study on 'Vengeance and Forgiveness', my heart sank, so black and bleak was the situation I was living in. I began to read these verses from Luke's Gospel. Through gritted teeth, I prayed blessings on my oppressor. Gradually hatred turned into a longing for the Lord to bring salvation and fill unmet needs. My anger dissipated.

After two long and painful years, we finally shared the Peace, awkwardly and formally. 'I really am a Christian now, I know you won't believe me but it's true.' I saw that it was true, because the gossip petered out, friends returned, and I was left to worship in that particular church in peace.

God's justice wasn't my idea of justice at all. It was so much better for both of us.

*Lord, help me to love my enemies,*
*bless those that curse me,*
*pray for those that spitefully use me*
*and, Lord, help me to forgive others as you have*
  *forgiven me.*

## Isaiah 42.1–3

Here is my servant, whom I uphold,
   my chosen, in whom my soul delights;
I have put my spirit upon him;
   he will bring forth justice to the nations.
He will not cry or lift up his voice,
   or make it heard in the street;
A bruised reed he will not break,
   and a dimly burning wick he will not quench;
He will faithfully bring forth justice.

In the eyes of the court justice had been done. The asylum seeker had been granted leave to stay in this country. And we celebrated together.

But then came the news. Now that he had been given permission to stay he would be relocated. With less than two days' notice, he was moved 270 miles away, to a town where he knew no one. And it was just a few weeks before Christmas.

Justice had been done. Only it didn't really feel like that.

Then God stepped in. Someone knew someone who was a Christian in the other town. Feeling like it was the only thing we could do, we managed to contact him. He and others from his church visited our friend, picked him up to take him to church, offered him hospitality and helped him to furnish his new flat. It was Christian love, God's love, in action.

And when I think of it, I'm reminded of how God's justice is different from the world's justice. He desires justice, but justice where bruised reeds are not broken, where dimly burning wicks are not quenched. And sometimes his justice is achieved without the lifting up of a voice but in the quiet, unnoticed actions of individuals.

*Lord God,*
*help me not to be content with the world's view of*
*justice.*
*Show me how to help to bring about your justice,*
*which shows love to those we so easily ignore.*

## Psalm 96.1–2, 10–13

O sing to the LORD a new song;
  sing to the LORD all the earth.
Sing to the LORD, bless his name;
  tell of his salvation from day to day.

Say among the nations, 'The LORD is king!
  The world is firmly established; it shall never be moved.
  He will judge the peoples with equity.'
Let the heavens be glad, and let the earth rejoice;
  let the sea roar, and all that fills it;
  let the field exult, and everything in it.
Then shall all the trees of the forest sing for joy
  before the LORD; for he is coming,
  for he is coming to judge the earth.
He will judge the world with righteousness,
  and the peoples with his truth.

It was a still, muggy night in early April in the south of France. We set off down the sandy track in our wellingtons, and entered the meadow. The sound was deafening. All around us, amorous amphibian music filled the air. Thousands of natterjack toads were singing their pulsating song, jostling for position in the shallow water. From the surrounding trees came the croaking chorus of stripeless tree frogs. And then another call, barely audible, but quite distinct – a single western spadefoot toad. She could have passed unnoticed, but, for those of us with ears to hear, her part in that nocturnal performance was thrilling.

So what do frogs and farmland have to do with God's desire for justice?

Psalm 96 calls the whole earth to sing to the Lord. This includes the non-human creation, in all its astonishing biodiversity. Sadly today, many of the virtuoso voices in creation's chorus are being muted. The spadefoot toad is now on the brink of extinction in France, after its dune habitats have all but been destroyed by tourist developments. Countless other species are threatened by intensive agriculture, water pollution and sprawling development.

God desires justice for his whole creation. The announcement of his coming judgement is therefore good news for the earth, which re-finds its voice and bursts into joyful song, anticipating God's great restoration of ecological harmony in the new creation.

Next time you're outside, listen for the voice of creation. Perhaps you'll hear a muffled cry for help. Or, just maybe, where the gospel is restoring relationships between people and their environment, you'll hear a new song of joy.

*Lord,*
*help me to listen and to hear.*

[ 9 ]

## Amos 5.21–24

I hate, I despise your festivals, and I take no delight in your solemn assemblies. Even though you offer me your burnt offerings and grain offerings, I will not accept them; and the offerings of well-being of your fatted animals I will not look upon. Take away from me the noise of your songs; I will not listen to the melody of your harps. But let justice roll down like waters, and righteousness like an ever-flowing stream.

When Amos looked around him, he could see all the outward signs of religion but, behind this, a deeply compromised people. They had lost their identity in God and had become caught up in the world around them. There was very little difference between the people of God and the world of oppression. Affluence, exploitation and the profit motive were the most notable features of society. There was immense commercial prosperity and an extremely wealthy aristocracy lived in extravagant opulence. On the other hand, the poor were extremely poor and shamelessly exploited. Society was structured in a way that kept the poor in destitution and, when they could no longer contribute to the rich, they were left and ignored.

A corrupt and uncaring, yet ostensibly religious, people were happy to live alongside injustice. That was not good enough for God in Amos's day and it's not good enough now. Food distribution programmes, bringing down evil regimes, education, sanitation or cancelling third world debt will not stop injustice (as important as they all are). You can't get rid of malaria by killing the mosquitoes; you get rid of it by destroying the swamps in which the mosquitoes breed – and the swamps that breed injustice are our hearts.

What Amos is saying is that our worship means nothing to God, no matter how good it sounds, if it's at the expense of the poor. If we do not have the poor at heart, our worship is not true worship. God demands that we be a people of spiritual renewal and compassion. We need to let God into our hearts to break them.

*Dear Lord, when our hearts have become hardened by the multiple overwhelming of poverty, war and global catastrophes, help us to allow you to soften them with your compassion.*

## Micah 6.6–8

'With what shall I come before the LORD,
   and bow myself before God on high?
Shall I come before him with burnt offerings,
   with calves a year old?
Will the LORD be pleased with thousands of rams,
   with ten thousands of rivers of oil?
Shall I give my firstborn for my transgression,
   the fruit of my body for the sin of my soul?'
He has told you, O mortal, what is good;
   and what does the LORD require of you
but to do justice, and to love kindness,
   and to walk humbly with your God?

We hear a lot about justice these days. It's on the TV and in the newspapers. 'Whose fault was it that ...?'; or, 'What are you going to do about it?' the TV journalist demands to know. Someone has to be blamed and punished for the terrible thing that has happened. We have a need to see 'justice' done. But whose justice is it to be? Is it my version, the journalist's, that of the popular press, or the view of some religious grouping?

And what do we mean by justice? Does it mean vengeance, or punishment, or simply a large slice of money for Messrs Sue, Grab-it & Run?

God's answer to Micah's question was that justice is bound up with kindness and walking with God. It comes as part of a package that cannot be separated or made to stand alone.

On the surface it looks easy until we look at the small print. Justice is to render to all their due. So we can punish them! Ah, but what about the next bit? We're called not only to perform acts of kindness but also to rejoice in every opportunity to do mercy and to be utterly dependent on God.

'Impossible!' we cry. No one has ever done that and it is just too much to ask anyone to do. Or is it? If we look to the cross, we see Jesus doing that for you and me.

We need God's justice for ourselves and to thank Jesus that he has shown justice to us so that we can show it to others. Who said following Jesus would be easy?

*Lord,*
*help me to read the small print,*
*to rejoice in doing mercy*
*and to be utterly dependent on you.*

[ 13 ]

## Genesis 9.8–17

Then God said to Noah and to his sons with him, 'As for me, I am establishing my covenant with you and your descendants after you, and with every living creature that is with you, the birds, the domestic animals, and every animal of the earth with you, as many as came out of the ark. I establish my covenant with you, that never again shall all flesh be cut off by the waters of a flood, and never again shall there be a flood to destroy the earth.' God said, 'This is the sign of the covenant that I make between me and you and every living creature that is with you, for all future generations: I have set my bow in the clouds, and it shall be a sign of the covenant between me and the earth. When I bring clouds over the earth and the bow is seen in the clouds, I will remember my covenant that is between me and you and every living creature of all flesh; and the waters shall never again become a flood to destroy all flesh. When the bow is in the clouds, I will see it and remember the everlasting covenant between God and every living creature of all flesh that is on the earth.' God said to Noah, 'This is the sign of the covenant that I have established between me and all flesh that is on the earth.'

We have been forced, over the past twenty-four months or so, to confront the destructive power of water: the tsunami in the Pacific, the hurricane-driven waves in the southern states of the USA, the mudslides caused by rain in Mexico and South America, icecaps melting at the Poles, even a torrential river in Boscastle, North Cornwall.

Maybe we can identify with Noah as he heard the command to build the ark and imagine the fear of those who were not on the ark as the flood waters rose.

It sounds like retributive justice: human beings messed up, so God punished them by drowning them and all the world. From an impersonal, purely objective view, we can call this justice. It's like a business arrangement: both sides have obligations, and if either side breaks the rules, the contract is terminated.

However, God is not an impersonal and disinterested God. He doesn't make contracts based on obligations and penalty clauses; he made a covenant based on love. And that means that, even if we mess up, we cannot undo the covenant. God is a personal God, who wants a relationship with his people, and so he continually offers the chance of renewal, a new start within an unchanging covenant of love. This is how God's justice differs from ours. We cannot remove ourselves from his justice, because we cannot remove ourselves from his love. That is why God requires justice for us, because he desires love for us.

*Lord God,*
*help me to hear your words of love*
*and turn back to your covenant of love.*

## Isaiah 30.18

Therefore the LORD waits to be gracious to you;
   therefore he will rise up to show mercy to you.
For the LORD is a God of justice;
   blessed are all those who wait for him.

I used to work in a profession which the outside world viewed with a curious mix of cynicism and expectation. An easy target for the butt of disparaging humour, but equally a place people often came to in need, hoping that somewhere lurking in the bowels of the legal system, justice was there to be found.

Despite my best intentions, some would leave from their encounter with the law more cynical than they arrived, others just bruised and disappointed. No doubt at times this was born of an imperfect system. But there was many an occasion when it was hard to avoid the feeling that expectations were unrealistic. The hopes of people embarking down the road of litigation varied immensely. Some sought self-preservation while others were happy to walk the high moral ground, hoping to make examples of unethical employers. But the world's justice often wasn't up to the job – hence the fertile ground for lawyer jokes!

In these words in Isaiah we are confronted with the God whose expression of justice is of a different scent. A justice that is suffused with grace and compassion, bound by a longing that we might know his love. A justice that finds its ultimate expression in the Son of God broken on a cross. A death that eternally weds justice to grace and compassion, so that life, and life to the full might be ours. Yes, we have a Lord of justice, but perhaps not as we might immediately anticipate.

*Lord,*
*help us to wait for you and on you,*
*so that we might know your perfect justice.*

## Jonah 2.6b–9

'Yet you brought up my life from the Pit,
   O Lord my God.
As my life was ebbing away,
   I remembered the Lord;
and my prayer came to you,
   into your holy temple.
Those who worship vain idols
   forsake their true loyalty.
But I with the voice of thanksgiving
   will sacrifice to you:
what I have vowed I will pay.
   Deliverance belongs to the Lord!'

In the Bible there are many stories of people questioning God's judgement because it seems unfair and unjust in their eyes. Many times they turn away from God, taking matters into their own hands, which results in further injustice and ruined lives. We see the victims become the victimisers, driven by anger and bitterness, and this leads to lives separated from God. Although the objective – to achieve justice – seems a good one, the outcome rarely is. Peace eludes them, anger and bitterness pulls them further from the source of peace – God.

God is both just and merciful. Consider Jonah – he clearly has a good relationship with God but runs away rather than confront the sinful people of Nineveh, perhaps waiting for God to pour out his judgement on them. It takes three days inside a fish before Jonah realizes his own disobedience, that he has run away from God and that he too needs forgiveness.

When a situation is unfair or when we are victims of others, let us remember that God is in charge. He loves justice and equity. Because of Jesus, we don't need to rely on ourselves. We have the living God who wants to work in our lives to bring about justice. He wants to involve us in his plan not just for our own sake but also for others. It is hard to let go of the hurt and let God lead us but, as we acknowledge our own need for forgiveness, it helps us to release that burden.

*Lord Jesus,*
*thank you for not giving up on me*
*when I turn away from you and do things my own*
  *way.*
*Help me to turn back to you*
*and trust that you will bring about justice your way.*

## Lamentations 3.21–26

But this I call to mind,
   and therefore I have hope:

The steadfast love of the LORD never ceases,
   his mercies never come to an end;
they are new every morning;
   great is your faithfulness.
'The LORD is my portion,' says my soul,
   'therefore I will hope in him.'

The LORD is good to those who wait for him,
   to the soul that seeks him.
It is good that one should wait quietly
   for the salvation of the LORD.

Earlier this week, I cycled into College on one of the coldest mornings of the year so far. Briefly facing east, I was greeted with the most spectacular sunrise, the sun a ball of fiery red piercing the dense fog, above white, dew-covered fields.

Like the writer of Lamentations, a refugee in a foreign land, we sometimes find ourselves in situations where God's presence seems totally absent. We live in a world where greed and selfishness lead to injustice and inequality – yet we are reminded, as the writer was, that God's love and faithfulness are as sure as the rising of the sun every day. Like the sun piercing the fog on that beautiful morning, God will always win through, no matter how gloomy things seem.

Perhaps you are in a situation full of bitterness and despair, where God seems to have abandoned you. Put your hope in him again today, because 'The Lord is good to those who wait for him'. If, on the other hand, you are already certain of God's faithfulness, then perhaps you know of someone who is struggling? Could you be God's instrument of hope to them today?

*Lord, make me an instrument of your peace;*
*where there is hatred, let me sow love;*
*where there is injury, pardon;*
*where there is doubt, faith;*
*where there is despair, hope;*
*where there is darkness, light;*
*and where there is sadness, joy.*

## Luke 4.16–21

When he came to Nazareth, where he had been brought up, he went to the synagogue on the Sabbath day, as was his custom. He stood up to read, and the scroll of the prophet Isaiah was given to him. He unrolled the scroll and found the place where it was written:

'The Spirit of the Lord is upon me, because he has anointed me to bring good news to the poor. He has sent me to proclaim release to the captives and recovery of sight to the blind, to let the oppressed go free, to proclaim the year of the Lord's favour.'

And he rolled up the scroll, gave it back to the attendant, and sat down. The eyes of all in the synagogue were fixed on him. Then he began to say to them, 'Today this scripture has been fulfilled in your hearing.'

I spent a number of years doing missionary work in India. I wanted to save people by proclaiming Christ's timeless call to conversion. I aimed to snatch people out of history and into eternity. Such things as caring for the oppressed and marginalized, perhaps by providing education and tackling socio-economic injustice, were a distraction best left to the State to look after. If such things were done by missionaries, I reasoned, it was with the aim of 'softening people up' to the real missionary task of proclaiming God's word about eternal salvation.

I much preferred reading the Great Commission of Matthew 28 rather than the passage from Luke's Gospel; when I did read the passage in Luke, I tended to 'spiritualize' the message. But believers in other parts of the world, particularly Latin America, challenged my view of salvation, with its emphasis on conversion as, in the words of Gustavo Gutiérrez, 'affected by the socio-economic, political, cultural and human environment in which it occurs. Without a change in these structures, there is no authentic conversion'. What a challenge! While I am still committed to Jesus' call to make disciples, I now realize it is only part of a much larger picture of what salvation means. And it is one thing to hear the cries from thousands of miles away, but what about injustice in our concrete historical circumstances?

*Heavenly Father,*
*give me the eyes to see the poor,*
*the marginalized*
*and the oppressed that surround me,*
*and soften my hard heart to respond.*

## Luke 23.35–43

And the people stood by, watching; but the leaders scoffed at him, saying, 'He saved others; let him save himself if he is the Messiah of God, his chosen one!' The soldiers also mocked him, coming up and offering him sour wine, and saying, 'If you are the King of the Jews, save yourself!' There was also an inscription over him, 'This is the King of the Jews.' One of the criminals who were hanged there kept deriding him and saying, 'Are you not the Messiah? Save yourself and us!' But the other rebuked him, saying, 'Do you not fear God, since you are under the same sentence of condemnation? And we indeed have been condemned justly, for we are getting what we deserve for our deeds, but this man has done nothing wrong.' Then he said, 'Jesus, remember me when you come into your kingdom.' He replied, 'Truly I tell you, today you will be with me in Paradise.'

I don't particularly enjoy it when people scoff at me because of my faith. I'm used to it by now, but that doesn't make it any easier to accept. It can be difficult to love the person who is mocking me. Sometimes, a desire for justice or revenge, perhaps by way of a cutting retort, comes to mind and I have to bite my tongue.

I can see too many reflections of my own past in the other person. Often in my absence from the Church in my twenties I would scoff at Christians. I was particularly scornful of those who sought God's provision in prayer. 'Surely God is too busy managing the universe to spend time finding you a job or healing you of a minor ailment', I argued. All too easily I can see myself among the crowds and with the first criminal deriding Jesus at his crucifixion.

But God does not seek revenge for my scoffing. Rather, God's greater sense of justice allowed Jesus to die on the cross. This allows me to share in the promise given to the second criminal of a place in Paradise.

Within our human limitations we are called to reflect back God's desire for justice to those we meet. Instead of going on the defensive, we are called to be compassionate and extend love to those who mock us.

*Heavenly Father,*
*help me to reflect your justice to those I meet,*
*including those who mock me for my faith in you.*

## Isaiah 58.6–11

Is not this the fast that I choose:
   to loose the bonds of injustice,
   to undo the thongs of the yoke,
to let the oppressed go free,
   and to break every yoke?
Is it not to share your bread with the hungry,
   and bring the homeless poor into your house;
when you see the naked, to cover them,
   and not to hide yourself from your own kin?
Then your light shall break forth like the dawn,
   and your healing shall spring up quickly;
your vindicator shall go before you,
   the glory of the LORD shall be your rear guard.
Then you shall call, and the LORD will answer;
   you shall cry for help, and he will say, Here I am.

If you remove the yoke from among you,
   the pointing of the finger, the speaking of evil,
if you offer your food to the hungry
   and satisfy the needs of the afflicted,
then your light shall rise in the darkness
   and your gloom be like the noonday.
The LORD will guide you continually,
   and satisfy your needs in parched places,
   and make your bones strong;
and you shall be like a watered garden,
   like a spring of water,
   whose waters never fail.

So many times Lent has come around and I have thought, 'What shall I give up this year?' Biscuits... chocolate... that'll help the waistline, or perhaps telly – but this crazy idea was soon shelved. I think that I have only once considered doing something, and that didn't last long at all!

I wonder why I should fast and give up something. Is it simply that I ought to? Will it make me feel better to give up a little thing and think that I am doing my part? Suddenly I am brought up short as I read what God considers as true fasting.

I have denied myself a little in past Lents, but I'm not sure if it has changed my heart, or caused me to consider how I could and should help others. Yet God expects me to feed the hungry, clothe the naked, free the oppressed, and fight against injustice. This is a huge, daunting and impossible task when viewed as a whole. But, if I consider only one person, then that is a start – the beginning of helping and changing one person's life.

So whether I give up chocolate, biscuits, meat, and give the money saved away to those who need it, or pray instead of eating a meal once a week, or write to those unjustly imprisoned, what matters is that my heart is changed; then I truly engage with God and begin to seek ways in which I can follow his desire for his world.

*Father,*
*open my eyes and let me see*
*where I can be your hands and voice.*
*Impassion my heart,*
*so that I can make a difference to peoples' lives,*
*and help your kingdom to be known on the earth.*

## Micah 6.8, NIV

And what does the LORD require of you? To act justly and to love mercy and to walk humbly with your God.

The Texan picked up his beer and leant along the bar. It was my first time in the States, and the notion of speaking to someone at random in a pub seemed odd; but it was commonplace over there, so we began to talk. We talked about the appointment of a new U.S. Chief Justice. Debates about the appointee were broadcast live on national television and it was an obvious choice of topic for conversation between two guys who met for the only time in a Virginia bar.

A new Chief Justice of England and Wales was also appointed this year. Unlike his American counterpart, ours of course will wear a wig and be called 'my Lord'! But the main difference is that there has been (in comparison with the American appointment) little fuss. What connects these appointments is that both societies value justice highly and make us all answerable to laws enforced in the courts.

And we are all – even the institutions of law themselves – ultimately answerable to God's justice. God's justice is absolute: absolute rightness, absolute justness. But it also embodies absolute love and absolute mercy. The balance between what is just and what is merciful is only possible for God; but our legal institutions are perhaps most godly when they strive to maintain that balance between the just and the merciful.

I'm not sure how this might look in practice. But perhaps we could begin by praying that those who administer justice may strive to reflect the justice which is higher than human justice, the mercy wider than human mercy, the love deeper than human love. I wonder what difference it would make if we all began to pray for our judges on a daily basis?

## Isaiah 55.8–9

For my thoughts are not your thoughts,
   nor are your ways my ways, says the Lord.
For as the heavens are higher than the earth,
   so are my ways higher than your ways
   and my thoughts than your thoughts.

I desire justice. Do *I*? If I'm truthful, I shrink from the reality of what justice might mean for me, whether as a Christian – I know there are many areas in which I would be judged wanting – or in material terms, fearful of what I might lose in a world where resources were more fairly distributed.

*I* fear justice. Yet I am drawn to the pictures Jesus sketched for us. Of God, who scatters the seed of his kingdom liberally, indiscriminately – whether on rocky ground or fertile soil; who pays his workers the whole day through – even though some arrived only close to evening; whose heart resounds with mercy as he forgives a servant's huge, unpayable debt; and who runs towards, and enfolds in his arms, the disgraced, hope-less prodigal son.

This justice – inseparably bonded with grace, love and mercy – takes my breath away. Would God do that for me? And am I willing to receive, to respond? Or like the prodigal's older sibling, will I sulk? Like the servant forgiven his debt, will I revert to a cold, human understanding of justice and menacingly demand debts from others?

Jesus opened the way for us to enter into God's amazing love, justice, mercy and grace. Slowly, I begin to comprehend that I do desire this justice – God's justice.

As I begin to take my first tentative, heartfelt steps of response, who knows? Perhaps that response – even if it seems such a small thing – might help someone else begin to experience God's loving justice as well.

*Father,*
*thank you that your ways are high above my ways.*
*Like the prodigal, help me to have the courage*
*to admit my brokenness and turn back to you.*

## 2 Samuel 12.7–10

Nathan said to David, 'You are the man! Thus says the LORD, the God of Israel: I anointed you king over Israel, and I rescued you from the hand of Saul; I gave you your master's house, and your master's wives into your bosom, and gave you the house of Israel and of Judah; and if that had been too little, I would have added as much more. Why have you despised the word of the LORD, to do what is evil in his sight? You have struck down Uriah the Hittite with the sword, and have taken his wife to be your wife, and have killed him with the sword of the Ammonites. Now therefore the sword shall never depart from your house, for you have despised me, and have taken the wife of Uriah the Hittite to be your wife.'

David had been chosen by God to be the king of his people Israel. God had promised that David's family would never die out and that there would always be a king of his line to rule over Israel. God had made David successful in all his battles from the time he confronted Goliath. God had done everything for David.

And David repaid God by committing adultery, killing a man, telling lies and ignoring God: four of the Ten Commandments broken.

If you were God, what would you do now? Break off relationships with David? Choose a new king? Abandon your promise to keep choosing kings from his family?

What God did was to send his Son, the redeemer of the world, to be born into David's family. Although that happened 1,000 years later, God kept his promise to David. Although David had sinned seriously against God and against his neighbour, God still gave him a second chance.

Sometimes we think that God's love is like a great big comfort blanket, in which we can wrap ourselves so that nothing hurts us. But that's not true love, because a comfort blanket can't face the truth. God's love is strong enough to face the truth about us and still to love us and keep his promises. That is why his love and his justice are linked. God's justice faces the truth and does not fear the consequences. God's love faces the consequences and still remains faithful to his promises. That is why, whatever happens, we can turn to him.

*Dear God,*
*help me to turn back to you when I stray,*
*to realize that your love is tough enough to cope with*
    *me*
*and that your justice is gentle enough to correct me.*

## 2 Corinthians 5.21

For our sake he made him to be sin who knew no sin, so that in him we might become the righteousness of God.

Thinking of justice, what springs immediately to my mind is the Fountain of Justice (or Righteousness) in Bern in Switzerland. This fountain depicts justice as a blindfolded woman holding a pair of scales in her hand.

When we think of justice, we think of an equal treatment for everybody without regard for the person. Justice is when I get what I deserve, when I am treated according to my deeds.

This stands in radical contrast to God's dealing with us as human beings. If God treated us according to our deeds, it would not look good at all. The scales would rapidly tell against us, for we have sinned and deserve to die.

God does not close his eyes and overlook our sins. He is a God that demands justice. But equally he is a loving God, who does not want any of his creatures to perish. Therefore God sent his Son into this world so that, in his death on the cross, the world might be reconciled to God. Jesus bore our sins and was judged in our place. He died so that we might be counted righteous in God's eyes and have life in abundance.

*Thank you God for Jesus*
*who fulfilled all righteousness*
*and reconciled us to you through*
*his death on the cross.*

## Isaiah 56.1–2

Thus says the LORD:
  Maintain justice, and do what is right,
for soon my salvation will come,
  and my deliverance be revealed.

Happy is the mortal who does this,
  the one who holds it fast,
who keeps the sabbath, not profaning it,
  and refrains from doing any evil.

## Luke 23.13–25

Pilate then called together the chief priests, the leaders, and the people, and said to them, 'You brought me this man as one who was perverting the people; and here I have examined him in your presence and have not found this man guilty of any of your charges against him. Neither has Herod, for he sent him back to us. Indeed, he has done nothing to deserve death. I will therefore have him flogged and release him.' Then they all shouted out together, 'Away with this fellow! Release Barabbas for us!' (This was a man who had been put in prison for an insurrection that had taken place in the city, and for murder.) Pilate, wanting to release Jesus, addressed them again; but they kept shouting, 'Crucify, crucify him!' A third time he said to them, 'Why, what evil has he done? I have found in him no ground for the sentence of death; I will therefore have him flogged and then release him.' But they kept urgently demanding with loud shouts that he should be crucified; and their voices prevailed. So Pilate gave his verdict that their demand should be granted. He released the man they asked for, the one who had been put in prison for insurrection and murder, and he handed Jesus over as they wished.

The lecturer in our class on Mark's Gospel directed us to look at Isaiah 55 to note the parallels between that and Mark 4. But, as had been my habit since a child at school, I kept reading the set text and found myself at these verses in Isaiah 56.

The biblical author starts a new theme with these verses, moving attention from the Israelites in exile and their redemption, to the homeland itself. Israel will be redeemed by God from corruption and ruin to be the centre of the earth, 'a crown of beauty'. God's covenant with Israel required his people to live justly, that is, according to the commandments given to them via Moses. 'Continue living in righteousness and treating all with justice', says God through Isaiah, 'because I am about to save you.'

The justice that Jesus teaches us in Mark and the other Gospels often seems an upside down or counter-intuitive justice when seen from our worldly view. But the world's justice and God's justice come together in one key event – the crucifixion. The salvation of Israel, and the rest of humanity, was achieved through human injustice. The corruption of worldly justice enabled the exercise of God's pure justice.

If Pilate had administered 'justice' and released Jesus, there would have been no crucifixion, no resurrection – and no salvation. But that act of injustice has enabled God to say to us, almost in the words of Isaiah, 'Maintain justice, and do what is right, for my salvation has come, and my deliverance has been revealed'.

*Lord Jesus,*
*thank you for being the means of our salvation.*
*Give us strength and courage in the sufferings of*
*injustice,*
*and the assurance that we are always part of your*
*kingdom.*

## Luke 15.25–32

'Now his elder son was in the field; and when he came and approached the house, he heard music and dancing. He called one of the slaves and asked what was going on. He replied, "Your brother has come, and your father has killed the fatted calf, because he has got him back safe and sound." Then he became angry and refused to go in. His father came out and began to plead with him. But he answered his father, "Listen! For all these years I have been working like a slave for you, and I have never disobeyed your command; yet you have never given me even a young goat so that I might celebrate with my friends. But when this son of yours came back, who has devoured your property with prostitutes, you killed the fatted calf for him!" Then the father said to him, "Son, you are always with me, and all that is mine is yours. But we had to celebrate and rejoice, because this brother of yours was dead and has come to life; he was lost and has been found." '

You only have to be around children for a short time before the whine 'It isn't fair' is heard, usually when a parent has exercised discipline or the desires of one child have been thwarted by another. I don't know the psychology involved, but a sense of fairness seems to be hardwired into us. We are very sensitive to the possibility of someone getting more than we do, more than their fair share. It just isn't fair that they earn more than we do for the same work, or there is more meat on their plate than on ours. Our idea of justice is that we all get an equal share.

The stay-at-home brother in the story of the prodigal son complains, 'It's not fair. You never gave me what you are giving my brother, and look what I have done for you compared with him! He's had his share already.' And, on the face of it, it isn't fair.

But this is not a story about fairness. The prodigal son deserved nothing from his father. He knew that and acknowledged it. His father showed him love, pity and grace – an echo of God's justice to us when we don't get it right, as we rarely do. Killing the fatted calf and celebrating was not fair. But it was a just response.

*Lord, I desire your justice, not fairness.*

## Psalm 74.9–17

We do not see our emblems;
   there is no longer any prophet,
   and there is no one among us who knows how long.
How long, O God, is the foe to scoff?
   Is the enemy to revile your name forever?
Why do you hold back your hand;
   why do you keep your hand in your bosom?
Yet God my King is from of old,
   working salvation in the earth.
You divided the sea by your might;
   you broke the heads of the dragons in the waters.
You crushed the heads of Leviathan;
   you gave him as food for the creatures of the wilderness.
You cut openings for springs and torrents;
   you dried up ever-flowing streams.
Yours is the day, yours also the night;
   you established the luminaries and the sun.
You have fixed all the bounds of the earth;
   you made summer and winter.

I am sure there have been times in all of our lives when we have desired justice. Further, I'm sure there have been times when we have identified with the Israelites in this psalm, when we have pleaded with God and despaired at how long he seems to allow injustices to continue apparently unnoticed. Also, there may have been times when the pressure was too great and we became the judge and delivered justice.

Yet Psalm 74 reminds us, firstly, that it is God who is the judge and, as a judge, his justice is based upon his sovereignty. He is God, who created life and time and who has the power and authority to overcome sickness and death and calm the natural world.

Secondly, this psalm reminds us that God's justice is intrinsically linked to his mercy. For, within the scales of God's justice, there is the weight of his mercy; a mercy which was evident as Abraham pleaded for the righteous in Sodom and Gomorrah; a mercy which was seen as Moses begged God not to destroy the Israelites after worshipping a golden calf; a mercy which was manifested at Mount Carmel as Elijah prayed to God to send the rains; a mercy which was demonstrated at the death of his Son on the cross; and a mercy which still exists today in each of our lives.

Finally, it's a mercy which holds back the gates of hell and the final judgement of the world in order to continue to offer salvation on this earth to us all.

*Father,*
*thank you that in your justice, there is mercy.*
*Help me to share the gospel with someone I meet*
  *today.*

## Mark 10.46–52

They came to Jericho. As he and his disciples and a large crowd were leaving Jericho, Bartimaeus son of Timaeus, a blind beggar, was sitting by the roadside. When he heard that it was Jesus of Nazareth, he began to shout out and say, 'Jesus, Son of David, have mercy on me!' Many sternly ordered him to be quiet, but he cried out even more loudly, 'Son of David, have mercy on me!' Jesus stood still and said, 'Call him here.' And they called the blind man, saying to him, 'Take heart; get up, he is calling you.' So throwing off his cloak, he sprang up and came to Jesus. Then Jesus said to him, 'What do you want me to do for you?' The blind man said to him, 'My teacher, let me see again.' Jesus said to him, 'Go; your faith has made you well.' Immediately he regained his sight and followed him on the way.

'Life has been interesting' is a description I frequently use to explain my journey of life from a child to an adult. Sometimes this is to evade the difficult questions about a past life which still holds many painful memories that have not yet been laid to rest with a finish and a flourish.

Life's journey is a road which is often set with obstacles, dips, potholes and even chasms. I have faced many myself. Some of the situations we find ourselves in seem plainly unfair.

The story of Bartimaeus shows that, if we have faith, we will receive justice and mercy. It would be a mistake to read this story as just another of Jesus' healings. Bartimaeus is not merely blind. He is a blind *beggar*. There was no social security system to help him out – he relied on the loudness of his voice to make his needs known. And people were clearly fed up with his haranguing them – they told him to shut up. Bartimaeus is socially isolated. But Jesus hears the desperation in the man's cry and insists on giving him a hearing. Crucially, he asks, 'What do you want me to do for you?' The answer may seem obvious, but sometimes individuals revel in their misery and even find their identity in it. Not so Bartimaeus: he was in no doubt he wanted his sight restored.

'Go; your faith has made you well.' If we cry out to Jesus in the midst of our difficulties, he will meet us. As with Bartimaeus, Jesus will respond to the injustice in our situation and mercifully meet us at our point of need.

*Lord,*
*help me to hear the cry of the social outcast*
*and give me the will to respond to it.*

## Deuteronomy 10.12–22

So now, O Israel, what does the LORD your God require of you? Only to fear the LORD your God, to walk in all his ways, to love him, to serve the LORD your God with all your heart and with all your soul, and to keep the commandments of the LORD your God and his decrees that I am commanding you today, for your own well-being. Although heaven and the heaven of heavens belong to the LORD your God, the earth with all that is in it, yet the LORD set his heart in love on your ancestors alone and chose you, their descendants after them, out of all the peoples, as it is today. Circumcise, then, the foreskin of your heart, and do not be stubborn any longer. For the LORD your God is God of gods and Lord of lords, the great God, mighty and awesome, who is not partial and takes no bribe, who executes justice for the orphan and the widow, and who loves the strangers, providing them food and clothing. You shall also love the stranger, for you were strangers in the land of Egypt. You shall fear the LORD your God; him alone you shall worship; to him you shall hold fast, and by his name you shall swear. He is your praise; he is your God, who has done for you these great and awesome things that your own eyes have seen. Your ancestors went down to Egypt seventy persons; and now the LORD your God has made you as numerous as the stars in heaven.

In this passage Moses is trying to remind the Israelites – not for the last time – to be faithful to the covenant that they have with God. The Israelites had quickly abandoned the commandments that Moses had brought down the mountain, and made the golden calf that they then worshipped. Moses had acknowledged to the Lord that his people were indeed guilty of sinning but pleaded with him to give them another chance. So the Lord re-inscribed the commandments and Moses again presented them to the Israelites.

Moses tells the Israelites that they are to walk in all God's ways, in the ways of a God who shows justice to the stranger, the poor, orphans and the widowed – to those who have not been dealt with fairly or are in need and trouble, the disadvantaged. In modern terms, we would probably describe this as the pursuit of 'social justice' – although arguably this may be tautologous because justice can only exist in a social context. It has no meaning except in relationship.

Jesus says, 'I give you a new commandment, that you love one another'. We exist in relationship with God and with each other, and one of the outworkings of being in such a relationship of love is the pursuit of justice. Indeed it is an imperative of a relationship of love. We cannot avoid it and remain true to our calling and covenant as Christians, any more than the Israelites could remain faithful to their covenant without walking in all God's ways.

*Jesus, please help me to walk in all your ways.*

## Psalm 98.1–4, 7–9

O sing to the LORD a new song,
  for he has done marvellous things.
His right hand and his holy arm
  have gained him victory.
The LORD has made known his victory;
  he has revealed his vindication in the sight of the
    nations.
He has remembered his steadfast love and faithfulness
  to the house of Israel.
All the ends of the earth have seen
  the victory of our God.
Make a joyful noise to the LORD, all the earth;
  break forth into joyous song and sing praises.

Let the sea roar, and all that fills it;
  the world and those who live in it.
Let the floods clap their hands;
  let the hills sing together for joy
at the presence of the LORD, for he is coming
  to judge the earth.
He will judge the world with righteousness,
  and the peoples with equity.

Have you ever had a speeding ticket? I'm ashamed to admit it, but I have. I desperately wanted to explain the extenuating circumstances but there didn't seem to be a box on the frighteningly official form for this. I just had to admit it and accept the punishment.

God's judgement can seem rather like this. We want to justify ourselves, or to hide from the truth. But surely God's standards are too high for this. He desires us to be perfect as he is perfect. 31 mph just isn't good enough. Salvation seems to be the opposite of this kind of judgement; as if it's another side of God's character; the forgiveness that we need to save us from his judgement.

But, thank God, this is a distortion of the truth. The psalmist saw judgement as a cause for rejoicing. He pictured all creation longing for God's judgement which can't contain its joy when God finally comes 'to judge the earth'.

This judgement isn't the fault-finding, legalistic process I'd feared. Instead, God judges wrong in order to free us from the tyranny of sin, both in us and against us. He doesn't give up on us when we mess up. We long for the injustice in the world to be righted, for all to be freed from poverty, oppression and hopelessness. But how much more does God long for this? And he is strong enough to bring about his justice and restore us, his beloved creation, to perfect joy and love in him.

*Holy God,*
*we long for you to restore this world.*
*Come swiftly with your judgement and your mercy.*

## Psalm 62.9–12

Those of low estate are but a breath,
    those of high estate are a delusion;
in the balances they go up;
    they are together lighter than a breath.
Put no confidence in extortion,
    and set no vain hopes on robbery;
    if riches increase, do not set your heart on them.

Once God has spoken;
    twice have I heard this:
that power belongs to God,
    and steadfast love belongs to you, O Lord.
For you repay to all
    according to their work.

On the cover of this book is a figure of Christ with a pair of scales, the traditional means of weighing an item by balancing it against a standard weight. I remember with delight visiting Greenwich market and seeing above one of the entrances 'A false balance is abomination to the LORD: but a just weight is his delight' (Proverbs 11.1). A deceitful trader could cunningly make a weight heavier or lighter to his advantage, but this proverb is a reminder that there is a judge on high, the Lord, who sees all and passionately desires justice and truth.

In the powerful image of Psalm 62, we too shall be weighed and assessed in the balance. But if so, how can we stand? As I look at the chaos of my life, the half-heartedness of my actions, my weaknesses, errors and sins, shall I not join those whom the psalmist sees going up in the air, lighter than a breath (the same word translated 'vanity' in Ecclesiastes)? Yet the psalmist retains his confidence in the Lord, whom he has affirmed is his rock, his salvation, and his refuge.

What makes the difference above all is the Lord's steadfast love. We are made to dwell and walk within this love and, as we do so (and only as we do so), our words and actions become more weighty and enduring than the purest of gold or the bluest of chips. As Christians, we have the assurance of forgiveness through Christ, and through the gift of the Holy Spirit we are able to live a life of faith that will not leave us ashamed on the last day.

*Lord,*
*grant me faith to put my trust entirely in you*
*and so not be found wanting*
*when my life is in your balance.*

## 1 Kings 21.17–22

Then the word of the LORD came to Elijah the Tishbite, saying: 'Go down to meet King Ahab of Israel, who rules in Samaria; he is now in the vineyard of Naboth, where he has gone to take possession. You shall say to him, "Thus says the LORD: Have you killed, and also taken possession?" You shall say to him, "Thus says the LORD: In the place where dogs licked up the blood of Naboth, dogs will also lick up your blood."'

Ahab said to Elijah, 'Have you found me, O my enemy?' He answered, 'I have found you. Because you have sold yourself to do what is evil in the sight of the LORD, I will bring disaster on you; I will consume you, and will cut off from Ahab every male, bond or free, in Israel; and I will make your house like the house of Jeroboam son of Nebat, and like the house of Baasha son of Ahijah, because you have provoked me to anger and have caused Israel to sin.'

This reading concludes the story of an ordinary person unjustly treated by the powerful, something that happens every day in our world. Yet Naboth's plight is not hidden from God's eyes. Not only does God see it, he is moved to do something about it, to do justice. He sends his prophet to challenge, and to pass sentence on, the perpetrators.

In the preceding passage, it is Ahab's wife Jezebel who plans and oversees the whole sorry episode. All Ahab does is to go and claim his glittering prize. But collection of that glittering prize is just as bad in God's eyes. It is the focus of the confrontation with the prophet, who stands in God's place. Ahab and his descendants will bear the just consequences of the unjust act, as indeed they do later.

This passage speaks to us today, too. Are we guilty of collecting our glittering prizes, gleaned through unjust acts? When we shop and buy products from sources which exploit other people, for example from child sweatshops, we too are sharing the guilt of those who are doing the exploiting. It behoves us, therefore, as far as we can, to be informed about the sources from which we buy. Ignorance is no excuse.

Far from colluding with the exploiters, may we have our eyes and ears open to the injustice that goes on around us; and let us stand in the tradition of the prophet to confront and challenge those who do the unjust exploiting.

*Almighty and just God,*
*grant us discernment not to collude with injustice*
*and courage to confront it.*

## John 3.16–17

For God so loved the world that he gave his only Son, so that everyone who believes in him may not perish but may have eternal life. Indeed, God did not send the Son into the world to condemn the world, but in order that the world might be saved through him.

I recently joined a rowing club to keep fit, get out in the open and meet some people outside of theological college.

One morning, after coaching some beginners, I rather reluctantly agreed to go for a drink with them – I was more focused on getting on with my day. As we started to talk, one of the guys told me that he had recently split up with his partner of eight years. A new man was already moving in with his former partner and their five-year-old daughter.

I wasn't expecting or wanting to hear what I was hearing, but I suddenly found myself face to face with the brokenness, lost-ness and pain of the world. I felt a deep sadness about the situation, love and compassion for all those involved and a desire for them all to know that there is a better way to live.

As we parted, I told him that I would be thinking of him. I hope and pray that I may have further opportunities to listen to him and gently direct him to the non-condemnatory, gracious and forgiving love of God and eternal life as found in his Son. Only with this love can broken and confused relationships be mended, healed, and reordered according to his perfect will.

*Lord God,*
*help us always to be willing and open to hear*
*the cries of the lost and broken*
*and to offer your words of salvation, hope and love.*

## Galatians 2.1–10

Then after fourteen years I went up again to Jerusalem with Barnabas, taking Titus along with me. I went up in response to a revelation. Then I laid before them (though only in a private meeting with the acknowledged leaders) the gospel that I proclaim among the Gentiles, in order to make sure that I was not running, or had not run, in vain. But even Titus, who was with me, was not compelled to be circumcised, though he was a Greek. But because of false believers secretly brought in, who slipped in to spy on the freedom we have in Christ Jesus, so that they might enslave us – we did not submit to them even for a moment, so that the truth of the gospel might always remain with you. And from those who were supposed to be acknowledged leaders (what they actually were makes no difference to me; God shows no partiality) – those leaders contributed nothing to me. On the contrary, when they saw that I had been entrusted with the gospel for the uncircumcised, just as Peter had been entrusted with the gospel for the circumcised (for he who worked through Peter making him an apostle to the circumcised also worked through me in sending me to the Gentiles), and when James and Cephas and John, who were acknowledged pillars, recognized the grace that had been given to me, they gave to Barnabas and me the right hand of fellowship, agreeing that we should go to the Gentiles and they to the circumcised. They asked only one thing, that we remember the poor, which was actually what I was eager to do.

Parting words often mean a lot, perhaps more than other parts of conversation. 'Remember to wash behind your ears!' as Mum watches her son leave home for far-flung places. 'I love you, so much' as both lovers try not to be the one who puts the phone down. 'Tell my kids how much I lo...' as the film star finally expires.

Imagine – Paul and Barnabas have travelled to Jerusalem to meet the elders of the Church. They have chewed over issues of law and the wonderful news that Gentiles were coming to faith. Then, having being welcomed into partnership to spread the gospel, the two apostles prepare to leave.

What would your advice have been? 'Don't neglect this doctrine, that practice, these values...' 'Remember to worship corporately, to read scripture publicly, to encourage prophecy, to celebrate the Eucharist.' But instead, with renewed vision, and apostolic authority, they walked from Jerusalem into persecutions and fruitful mission, with the words 'Remember the poor' ringing in their ears.

All they asked was that we continue to remember the poor. Why that advice? Why those parting words? Perhaps because the poor are the people we most easily forget.

What is almost more amazing is Paul's response. He was eager to remember the poor. Of all the hopes, plans, fears and uncertainties Paul must have had whirling around, he was sure he would not forget those who are so easily forgotten.

*Lord Jesus Christ, who walked with, and loved, those whom others would rather have forgotten, help me to follow the example of St Paul today. Show me how I can become someone who does not forget the poor. Enable me, by the power of your Holy Spirit, to have eyes to see those whom you see and to love them.*

## Revelation 7.9–17

After this I looked, and there was a great multitude that no one could count, from every nation, from all tribes and peoples and languages, standing before the throne and before the Lamb, robed in white, with palm branches in their hands.

> They cried out in a loud voice, saying,
> 'Salvation belongs to our God who is
> seated on the throne, and to the Lamb!'

And all the angels stood around the throne and around the elders and the four living creatures, and they fell on their faces before the throne and worshipped God, singing,

> 'Amen! Blessing and glory and wisdom
> and thanksgiving and honour
> and power and might
> be to our God for ever and ever! Amen.'

Then one of the elders addressed me, saying, 'Who are these, robed in white, and where have they come from?' I said to him, 'Sir, you are the one that knows.' Then he said to me, 'These are they who have come out of the great ordeal; they have washed their robes and made them white in the blood of the Lamb. For this reason they are before the throne of God, and worship him day and night within his temple, and the one who is seated on the throne will shelter them. They will hunger no more, and thirst no more; the sun will not strike them, nor any scorching heat; for the Lamb at the centre of the throne will be their shepherd, and he will guide them to springs of the water of life, and God will wipe away every tear from their eyes.'

I had the privilege of living in Cairo where I witnessed God's justice being worked out through Refuge Egypt, a refugee programme of the Episcopal Cathedral.

Let me share an incident related by Dr Keith, who was asked by UNHCR to verify the story of a Somali youth who alleged that a mortar had left him deaf and mute. The interpreter was an older relative who had been shot in the mouth while in detention and had lost his lower jaw. He was able to understand the young man but communicated with signs that Keith couldn't decipher. A third man was called who spoke English; he could understand the signing but had no arms. Keith's interview was relayed through three victims of conflict. A ripple of laughter spread between the four men as they recognized the absurdity of the situation. Working as an agent of God's reconciliation and justice is a powerful witness to God's love. A Sudanese wept as he spoke of the trust and acceptance he witnessed in the refugee programme that he had not experienced in his homeland.

Working for justice involves struggling towards restoration of relationships; between God and humanity and within human society. It is this reconciliation Christ came to bring about through the cross. Today's verses from Revelation look forward to that day when God's justice will finally, publicly and universally be established for people of every tribe and tongue. It is not through blood spilt in conflict that justice will ultimately be established but through the 'blood of the Lamb'. Then God will wipe away every tear from their eyes.

*Lord,*
*we pray for justice here on earth,*
*for relationships to be restored,*
*for right to prevail and for your wholeness*
*and healing to restore that which is damaged.*

## Luke 6.20–21

Then [Jesus] looked up at his disciples and said:
   'Blessed are you who are poor,
     for yours is the kingdom of God.
   Blessed are you who hunger now,
     for you will be filled.
   Blessed are you who weep now,
     for you will laugh.'

Poverty. We know it's there, but mostly it's far enough away that we can keep its disturbing truth at arm's length.

A visit to a diocese in West Africa showed me a snapshot of what poverty can look like. Over my three-week visit, I was blessed by the chance to spend time chatting and laughing with African friends who were full of the love of God, and together we celebrated the joy of Jesus' risen presence in our midst. Yet for these brothers and sisters, the reality of poverty meant that on some days there wasn't any food, so they didn't eat.

I returned to England keen to help, having established the appropriate ways of supporting the ministries and communities that I had visited. But a couple of months later and it just seemed to have slipped out of my mind. My enthusiastic commitment to living out justice for the poor in my own life, with my own budget, became just a passing whim, a nice idea, which failed to materialize in the cold light of day.

My heart is selfish, and my generosity towards those in need is fickle. Writing this reflection has reminded me of how God challenged me through visiting the Christians in West Africa. That has renewed my commitment to share something of what I have with them.

The compassionate heart of God is with the poor, and he will establish justice in his kingdom.

*Lord, may your kingdom come,*
*on the earth,*
*in my life,*
*as in heaven.*

DAY 30 – WEEK 5 – THURSDAY

## Micah 6.8b

And what does the LORD require of you, but to do justice…

The prophets are crystal clear: God's passion for justice is deep and true, and requires his people to act appropriately. Whether we consult Amos, Isaiah or Jeremiah, the Lord's non-negotiable insistence on good practice in all human relationships and social structures is both fundamental and inescapable.

Of course the Lord Jesus himself, the greatest of prophets, announced justice 'to the nations'. And, indeed, as the New Testament foresees earthly history reaching towards its climax, all arenas of politics, commerce and consumption are enveloped by this great and enduring concern.

As followers and friends of Jesus Christ, justice is something we simply have to 'do'. It is to operate on the level of action and lifestyle. Our affairs have to be ordered in a way that consciously pursues peace and purposefully avoids inflicting abuse or distress. We can try, for instance, to arrange our personal finances carefully, so that money for which we are responsible is managed wisely and fairly, without participation in the evils of oppression or needless pollution.

Ultimately, justice will not pervade our buying and selling, our work and leisure, our eating and drinking, until, by God's grace, we become people who are clothed with compassion. For justice is a fruit of compassion. And compassion is a quality, rooted in the heart of God, that has to be intelligently and deliberately cultivated.

*Heavenly Father,*
*give me the grace to communicate your compassion*
*to people who suffer.*

## Romans 8.18–25

I consider that the sufferings of this present time are not worth comparing with the glory about to be revealed to us. For the creation waits with eager longing for the revealing of the children of God; for the creation was subjected to futility, not of its own will but by the will of the one who subjected it, in hope that the creation itself will be set free from its bondage to decay and will obtain the freedom of the glory of the children of God. We know that the whole creation has been groaning in labour pains until now; and not only the creation, but we ourselves, who have the first fruits of the Spirit, groan inwardly while we wait for adoption, the redemption of our bodies. For in hope we are saved. Now hope that is seen is not hope. For who hopes for what is seen? But if we hope for what we do not see, we wait for it with patience.

When working abroad, I attended a meeting of local charities who wanted to challenge the government about the lack of citizens' rights. The discussion led to an expectation that life should be as 'free' as it is in the 'west'. I reminded the meeting that freedom and rights had always come at a cost to those seeking them. I spoke of the history of the 'west' and suggested that it had often taken, and still did take, decades for governments to reform.

In a second incident a boy was caught in the cross-fire between local police and a mob, while walking home to collect his school books. The police were using exorbitant force and the boy was beaten and taken to prison miles from home. I spent days trying to get the boy released from detention. We had regular meetings with the police urging them to be more mindful of children. Although we managed to get them to place children's officers in each police station, such incidents continued to happen.

Justice doesn't just happen. The world and its structures are often opposed to justice. It is obtained by patience, perseverance and a sense of hope. Paul writes that the whole of creation groans.

We live as Christians in a time when we see the first-fruits of the Spirit working in our lives, but we have not got to the place of completion. This is the time of tension when the kingdom of God is here, but not fully here. Let us groan with creation in prayer as we cry out 'your kingdom come, your will be done.'

*Father,*
*may your kingdom come,*
*and your will be done on earth, as in heaven.*

## Isaiah 1.10–11, 18–20

Hear the word of the LORD,
    you rulers of Sodom!
Listen to the teaching of our God,
    you people of Gomorrah!
What to me is the multitude of your sacrifices?
    says the LORD;
I have had enough of burnt offerings of rams
    and the fat of fed beasts;
I do not delight in the blood of bulls,
    or of lambs, or of goats.

Come now, let us argue it out,
    says the LORD:
though your sins are like scarlet,
    they shall be like snow;
though they are red like crimson,
    they shall become like wool.
If you are willing and obedient,
    you shall eat the good of the land;
but if you refuse and rebel,
    you shall be devoured by the sword;
    for the mouth of the LORD has spoken.

I was once part of a church leadership team which was trying to decide on a new logo for the church we were leading. Sadly, the logo design and review process degenerated into a protracted series of often bitter disagreements, marked more by individual agendas than by the need for the church to have an appropriate logo to help make us known in the community and further God's kingdom. As a leadership team, we had lost sight of the core of God's call to love him with all our hearts and to love each other correspondingly.

Isaiah tells us that God is calling his people to repent from treating each other in unjust ways, to return to his priorities of love and care and to receive his unearned forgiveness.

Today, you and I may not be fighting with others over a logo or feel we are neglecting the weak and needy within our church families. Do we really seek to give the all-consuming love of God to all the members of God's family? Through Jesus we can come and have our 'scarlet sins' washed to be 'white as snow'. Through the Holy Spirit we can love more, even those who prefer a different logo.

*Heavenly Father,*
*through Jesus and the prophets*
*you call us to love one another.*
*Help me to love all your family*
*through Jesus Christ, who loves us all.*

## John 8.3–11

The scribes and the Pharisees brought a woman who had been caught in adultery; and making her stand before all of them, they said to [Jesus], 'Teacher, this woman was caught in the very act of committing adultery. Now in the law Moses commanded us to stone such women. Now what do you say?'

They said this to test him, so that they might have some charge to bring against him. Jesus bent down and wrote with his finger on the ground. When they kept on questioning him, he straightened up and said to them, 'Let anyone among you who is without sin be the first to throw a stone at her.'

And once again he bent down and wrote on the ground. When they heard it, they went away, one by one, beginning with the elders; and Jesus was left alone with the woman standing before him. Jesus straightened up and said to her, 'Woman, where are they? Has no one condemned you?' She said, 'No one, sir.' And Jesus said, 'Neither do I condemn you. Go your way, and from now on do not sin again.'

How many times have I mentally passed judgement on others? Made assumptions? Jumped to conclusions?

I wonder how the gathered crowd would have viewed this woman, hauled humiliatingly before Jesus by the teachers of the law and the Pharisees? Perhaps they saw her as that wayward woman warned of in Proverbs deserving punishment.

And the adulteress? What might have been going through her mind? Did she feel a sense of shame? Humiliation? Anger? Fear? And what about the other party, the man. Was he watching too?

It is for good reason we are commanded not to judge others. There are at least two sides to every story.

How reassuring that our Lord is gracious to us. He passed no judgement on this woman. Disqualified by their own sinfulness, her earthly accusers went away, one by one, until only Jesus was left. He asked her: 'Woman, where are they? Has no one condemned you?' She said, 'No one, sir.' And Jesus said, 'Neither do I condemn you. Go away, and from now on do not sin again.'

I hear him ask the same of me.

*Gracious God,*
*thank you that you know my heart and judge me fairly.*
*Grant me the humility to leave the judgement of others*
*to you also.*

## Isaiah 1.27–28; 2.2–4

Zion shall be redeemed by justice, and those in her who repent, by righteousness. But rebels and sinners shall be destroyed together, and those who forsake the LORD shall be consumed.

In days to come the mountain of the LORD's house shall be established as the highest of the mountains, and shall be raised above the hills; all the nations shall stream to it. Many peoples shall come and say, 'Come, let us go up to the mountain of the LORD, to the house of the God of Jacob; that he may teach us his ways and that we may walk in his paths.' For out of Zion shall go forth instruction, and the word of the LORD from Jerusalem. He shall judge between the nations, and shall arbitrate for many peoples; they shall beat their swords into ploughshares, and their spears into pruning hooks; nation shall not lift up sword against nation, neither shall they learn war any more.

I was fortunate enough to spend three weeks in the Holy Land in July. It was in many ways a wonderful time – to be able to visit biblical sites, to walk where Jesus and his disciples walked and to see some, at least, of the same landscapes as they saw, brings the Bible to life in a unique way.

We also saw modern Israel and Palestine, an experience which shed a different light on the visit. From our place of morning prayer in the garden we could see into Bethlehem, and the eight-metre-high wall being built around it in order to stop terrorist attacks. And we could see, and visit, the prison that it made of the town. We were never quite sure if the noises we heard at night were fireworks or shots. Wherever we went in Jerusalem we were reminded of the crisis.

This passage from Isaiah is part of a section telling about a crisis facing Zion (Jerusalem), and is followed by a prophecy of the judgement of God issued from the city, 'the highest of the mountains' and 'the Lord's house'. But the justice administered is God's justice, containing both fiery love and merciful judgement.

The solution to the current crisis in the country is not an easy one; there are rights and wrongs on both sides. Justice seems all too human in modern Zion, and the redemption of the city and its people a distant possibility. Pray that Isaiah's prophecy of God's justice will be fulfilled again in our time.

*Lord,*
*help all those in Israel and Palestine*
*to treat each other with fiery love and merciful*
*judgement,*
*so that nation shall no longer fight against nation*
*and your peace shall reign.*

## Matthew 5.3–12

'Blessed are the poor in spirit, for theirs is the kingdom of
  heaven.
Blessed are those who mourn, for they will be comforted.
Blessed are the meek, for they will inherit the earth.
Blessed are those who hunger and thirst for righteousness,
  for they will be filled.
Blessed are the merciful, for they will receive mercy.
Blessed are the pure in heart, for they will see God.
Blessed are the peacemakers, for they will be called
  children of God.
Blessed are those who are persecuted for righteousness'
  sake, for theirs is the kingdom of heaven.
Blessed are you when people revile you and persecute
  you and utter all kinds of evil against you falsely on
  my account. Rejoice and be glad, for your reward is
  great in heaven, for in the same way they persecuted the
  prophets who were before you.'

When Jesus said that those who were suffering were truly blessed, I wonder what his audience thought. What do you think? Was it some cynical move to keep the masses quiet in their servitude, with the promise of pie in the sky when you die? If that were all Jesus was offering, it would not speak highly of God's justice.

God, who made the world to be good and fruitful, cannot be satisfied when he sees his people going without and suffering. That is not justice. But this list of blessings does indicate something about God's justice.

God's justice is all-consuming and all-encompassing for those who seek it.

Those people who are blessed have nothing from the world, so they are open to everything from God. The key to understanding this is verse 11: people are blessed when they suffer for Jesus' sake. When we give up everything to Jesus and everything for Jesus, then we have our hands free to receive everything from Jesus.

God's justice is not pie in the sky when you die, but the outpouring of his blessing now for those who will open their hands to receive it.

If we want to receive God's justice, we need to ask, 'What are the things in this world that we are hanging on to too tightly?' and let go of them so that we might truly have a free hand for God's blessings.

*O God,*
*you are just and merciful to give us what we need.*
*Give us the desire to lay aside everything for your sake*
*and open hands to receive you in our lives.*

## Matthew 20.1–16

'For the kingdom of heaven is like a landowner who went out early in the morning to hire labourers for his vineyard. After agreeing with the labourers for the usual daily wage, he sent them into his vineyard. When he went out about nine o'clock, he saw others standing idle in the market-place; and he said to them, "You also go into the vineyard, and I will pay you whatever is right." So they went. When he went out again about noon and about three o'clock, he did the same. And about five o'clock he went out and found others standing around; and he said to them, "Why are you standing here idle all day?" They said to him, "Because no one has hired us." He said to them, "You also go into the vineyard." When evening came, the owner of the vineyard said to his manager, "Call the labourers and give them their pay, beginning with the last and then going to the first." When those hired about five o'clock came, each of them received the usual daily wage. Now when the first came, they thought they would receive more; but each of them also received the usual daily wage. And when they received it, they grumbled against the landowner, saying, "These last worked only one hour, and you have made them equal to us who have borne the burden of the day and the scorching heat." But he replied to one of them, "Friend, I am doing you no wrong; did you not agree with me for the usual daily wage? Take what belongs to you and go; I choose to give to this last the same as I give to you. Am I not allowed to do what I choose with what belongs to me? Or are you envious because I am generous?" So the last will be first, and the first will be last.'

'It's not fair!'

It's the indignant cry every parent must have heard many times as their children grow up. From a very young age we learn to measure against others what we have and what we do. Your little brother comes home clutching a pound coin which he has been given just for looking cute. 'It's not fair!' It's not fair when we have to do the washing up, fetch the milk, or tidy the house when it's not our turn. When those around us seem to get away with doing little when we work so hard or when they have all the blessings – the beautiful house, an amazing voice, good looks – it offends our sense of justice.

Do we compare what we receive with others? Do we find ourselves crying 'It's not fair' when we see God's love and generosity extended to those whom we see as less worthy than ourselves?

We need to take some time to think of the issues that make us think life is unfair. Are we holding on to an 'injustice' that is making us bitter? God's justice may surprise us. He doesn't operate a points system.

Jesus turns our narrow human concept of justice upside down. All the workers are paid the same regardless of how long or hard they worked, and those who should have received their pay last, he paid first.

Jesus says this is what the kingdom of heaven is like. We aren't paid according to our works, thank goodness – who of us would be worthy? Instead, God's bigger justice will break through. His abundant generosity will be poured out on all who receive his invitation.

*Lord Jesus,*
*thank you that you are abundantly generous.*
*Help me to stop worrying about what is fair*
*and to rely on your mercy.*

[ 73 ]

## Proverbs 5.21

For human ways are under the eyes of the LORD,
  and he examines all their paths.

My mother often laughs about an incident, which occurred at a launderette when I was three and a half and my younger brother was small enough to be in a pushchair, but old enough to eat crisps.

Mum had given each of us a packet to keep us happy while she emptied an industrial-sized drier. Being small, my brother only managed one or two of his crisps in the time it took me to polish mine off. With Mum's back turned and the empty packet rustling in my hand, I had a sudden stroke of inspiration.

I began to dip my hand into my brother's packet and transfer the contents into my bag. I realized, that if I stocked up quickly enough, I'd be able to eat at leisure with Mum none the wiser. A whole packet seemed to be wasted on my brother, and anyway he couldn't speak yet so the incident would remain our little secret.

I was almost done when I chanced to glance in my mother's direction and found her staring straight at me. Without a word passing between us, I immediately transferred all the crisps back into my brother's packet, sat down and began to study the floor at some length.

Individuals (even Christians), governments and global corporations are often tempted to take advantage of the weak and voiceless. Justice demands that we remember that our deeds are under the eyes of God and we need to act accordingly.

*Heavenly Father,*
*you know everything that is in our hearts*
*and see everything that we do.*
*Strengthen us to resist the temptation*
*to exploit the weak and voiceless and to help them*
*    instead.*

## John 5.1–9a

After this there was a festival of the Jews, and Jesus went up to Jerusalem. Now in Jerusalem by the Sheep Gate there is a pool, called in Hebrew Bethzatha, which has five porticoes. In these lay many invalids – blind, lame, and paralysed. One man was there who had been ill for thirty-eight years. When Jesus saw him lying there and knew that he had been there a long time, he said to him, 'Do you want to be made well?' The sick man answered him, 'Sir, I have no one to put me into the pool when the water is stirred up; and while I am making my way, someone else steps down ahead of me.' Jesus said to him, 'Stand up, take your mat and walk.' At once the man was made well, and he took up his mat and began to walk.

This man had suffered for thirty-eight years! He spent each day at a pool that was said to have healing powers, but he never was healed. Someone always got into the water before him and that wasn't fair. He needed someone to help him, but there was nobody who would and that really wasn't just.

But Jesus saw him, knew him, loved him and wanted to make him whole. If this man thought that getting into the pool was his only chance of getting well, Jesus tipped his ideas upside down by offering a different kind of healing. Jesus healed him with a simple command: 'Stand up, take your mat and walk.'

There lies the difference. Only one person at a time could be healed in the pool and only when the water was stirred up. The period for healing was strictly limited. No doubt superstition may have played a part.

Jesus saw the injustice of the situation and acted immediately. His healing was the work of a merciful God. God's justice and mercy were accessible to the person at the pool and are accessible to us.

What are the things that we need Jesus to recognize in us so that he draws alongside us and asks, 'Do you want to be made well?' Past hurts, illness, frustrations, losses? Where do you need God's mercy?

Are you sitting at the edge of the pool, losing hope? Jesus sees you, loves you, knows you and wants you to receive God's mercy.

*Lord Jesus,*
*thank you that you know us so well*
*and that your love for us is unending.*
*As we come to you today,*
*may we know your healing and wholeness in a new*
*    way.*

## Deuteronomy 7.6–11

For you are a people holy to the LORD your God; the LORD your God has chosen you out of all the peoples on earth to be his people, his treasured possession. It was not because you were more numerous than any other people that the LORD set his heart on you and chose you – for you were the fewest of all peoples. It was because the LORD loved you and kept the oath that he swore to your ancestors, that the LORD has brought you out with a mighty hand, and redeemed you from the house of slavery, from the hand of Pharaoh king of Egypt. Know therefore that the LORD your God is God, the faithful God who maintains covenant loyalty with those who love him and keep his commandments, to a thousand generations, and who repays in their own person those who reject him. He does not delay but repays in their own person those who reject him. Therefore, observe diligently the commandment – the statutes, and the ordinances – that I am commanding you today.

How often our demand for justice is inversely proportionate to our proximity to those suffering injustice!

When we see images of starving children in drought-ridden, war-torn, debt-burdened countries thousands of miles from us, we demand justice. We rail at the television news, write to our MP, put on a white wristband – anything to indicate our desire for justice. When a friend loses a job, a relation contracts a terrible disease, a local child is killed in a road accident, we ask why the innocent suffer unjustly.

Maybe that is why, when it comes to ourselves, we often fear justice. If justice means receiving our just deserts, what do we deserve from God? If God is just and metes out justice, our just deserts would be punishment, for we are not good or innocent. But that is to misunderstand God's justice.

In today's reading, Moses is reporting why God rescued the Israelites from Egypt and brought them to the promised land. It wasn't because they deserved it, nor because they were big, clever or good, but just because he had set his heart on them, because he loved them. God rescued his people not because they deserved justice, but because he is just.

God's justice means that, whatever we have done, whatever 'just deserts' we deserve, he wants to give us his justice. His love will remove the stains of our injustice and his Spirit will renew us for just living.

God's justice lies not in giving us our just deserts, but loving us back into his just ways.

*Faithful God,*
*your love for me is so great, I scarcely dare believe it.*
*Repeat your call of love to my fearful heart,*
*so that I may trust your promises and dare to love you*
   *too.*

## 1 Thessalonians 5.16–28

Rejoice always, pray without ceasing, give thanks in all circumstances; for this is the will of God in Christ Jesus for you.

Do not quench the Spirit. Do not despise the words of prophets, but test everything; hold fast to what is good; abstain from every form of evil.

May the God of peace himself sanctify you entirely; and may your spirit and soul and body be kept sound and blameless at the coming of our Lord Jesus Christ. The one who calls you is faithful, and he will do this.

Beloved, pray for us.

Greet all the brothers and sisters with a holy kiss. I solemnly command you by the Lord that this letter be read to all of them.

The grace of our Lord Jesus Christ be with you.

This passage vividly evokes for me an evening church meeting in mid-Essex and a Romanian lay pastor.

Through *Aid to Russian Christians*, which operated throughout the eastern bloc countries, we had written to Pavel for some years using a postal method that required a receipt. We then knew if our Christian brother under communist rule was still alive and, hopefully, free.

With the fall of the communist-backed regime in Romania, Pavel had come to England to meet with his supporters.

We were treated to an evening of wonderful evangelistic enthusiasm from a man who had been tortured, had his flat burned out, been hounded by the authorities and whose family had been under constant threat. He particularly encouraged us to greet each other with a holy kiss – and in the wake of his infectious zeal, several of us cast off our 'normal' reserve and a sense of deep fellowship pervaded the evening. It was difficult to describe, almost tangible.

Now, more than a decade later, Pavel is involved in regular missions to Moldova, where poverty is endemic. That fervour we witnessed in Essex is being turned to astonishing account: meetings where huge numbers of people turn to Jesus. Hope germinates.

Pavel is able to empathize with the Moldovans' suffering because of his own tribulations. It is as if God is redeeming the awful injustices of his past with the gift of new souls for the kingdom.

*Dear God,*
*We praise and thank you*
*that you bring blessings from our brokenness.*

## Romans 6.20–23

When you were slaves of sin, you were free in regard to
righteousness. So what advantage did you then get from the
things of which you now are ashamed? The end of those
things is death. But now that you have been freed from sin
and enslaved to God, the advantage you get is sanctifica-
tion. The end is eternal life. For the wages of sin is death,
but the free gift of God is eternal life in Christ Jesus our
Lord.

Justice and loyalty go hand in hand. To make sure we remain loyal in our shopping, supermarkets offer loyalty cards with reward points. Now there's justice – if we spend enough, we'll get a reward.

In Romans 6, we are reminded that our misplaced loyalty was to sin. Sin offered us a loyalty card, which stacked up reward points alienating us from God and bringing us closer to the final reward of death. We were fully hooked into the system. But sin isn't worth our loyalty.

God's justice is freeing and rewards us with life. When Jesus passed into death and came out on the other side, he broke sin's power to demand our loyalty and hold us with false rewards. Sin can no longer be our master if we accept Jesus as our master.

Justice demands that we remain loyal to our new master. God has given us a loyalty card fully charged with reward points called justification. We don't need to keep on spending to get more and, rather than redeeming the points, the points redeem us. With a Jesus loyalty card, we are given freedom from slavery and from loyalty to sin. Now justice demands that we keep using our Jesus loyalty card to remain loyal to God.

*Almighty God,*
*pour out your Spirit on me*
*to give me strength to cut up my old sin loyalty card*
*and to receive my Jesus loyalty card*
*which you have charged with the free gift of eternal*
*life.*
*Help me today, and every day, to live in this new life.*

## Jeremiah 22.1–3

Thus says the LORD: Go down to the house of the king of Judah, and speak there this word, and say: Hear the word of the LORD, O King of Judah sitting on the throne of David – you, and your servants, and your people who enter these gates. Thus says the LORD: Act with justice and righteousness, and deliver from the hand of the oppressor anyone who has been robbed. And do no wrong or violence to the alien, the orphan, and the widow, or shed innocent blood in this place.

Slavery is sadly not just a part of our history but also a present reality. According to Anti-Slavery International, millions of men, women and children around the world are forced to lead lives as slaves. Although this exploitation is often not called slavery, the conditions are the same. People are sold like objects, forced to work for little or no pay and are at the mercy of their 'employers'. I was particularly shocked to discover that over eight million children worldwide are in slavery, trafficking, debt bondage and other forms of forced labour, forced recruitment for armed conflict, prostitution, pornography and other illicit activities (www.antislavery.org).

Where is justice for these children who have been robbed of their childhood? Who can and will speak out on their behalf? As Christians we have a responsibility to take seriously all injustice, including slavery in all its forms, and to act on behalf of those who are unable to act for themselves.

It is so much easier to do nothing, to ignore the victims of oppression and continue with our lives as though all was well. But all is not well. Elie Wiesel, a survivor of the Holocaust, poignantly reminds us in one of his poems that indifference is the opposite of love, faith and life. How easy it is for us to be indifferent, with potentially devastating consequences.

God desires us to act with justice and righteousness. One way of helping today, perhaps, would be to join a pressure group to help alleviate the injustice of slavery in our world.

*God of justice,*
*forgive us for when we have chosen an easy life by*
    *ignoring injustice.*
*Challenge our indifference*
*and give us wisdom,*
*that we may bring your justice and righteousness*
*to those who are trapped in oppression and exploitation.*

## Luke 16.25–26

'But Abraham said, "Child, remember that during your lifetime you received your good things, and Lazarus in like manner evil things; but now he is comforted here, and you are in agony. Besides all this, between you and us a great chasm has been fixed, so that those who might want to pass from here to you cannot do so, and no one can cross from there to us." '

It had been raining and there was a sharp wind. It was getting late and the streets were quiet, dimly lit. It was bitterly cold and I was hurrying home to the warmth of my fireside.

Then I saw him, curled up in a doorway, cardboard for a makeshift mattress and wind-break, a blanket his only, inadequate, protection. A dog lay beside him – his faithful companion.

I stopped, uncertain of what to do. I shuffled my feet nervously and pretended to look at the display in a nearby shop-window. My head raced. Should I try to help? No, the man was probably high on drink or drugs – it was obviously his fault that he was in that condition. But what if he was ill? Well, the State would look after him.

My train of thought was broken as a van pulled up. A man and a woman got out. They went straight over to the doorway and knelt down. I watched, fascinated. A few moments later and they were helping the man to his feet and into the van, along with his dog and few belongings. As they drove off, I noticed the name on the van, a Christian organization with a hostel in the town.

I felt ashamed. In spite of my relative affluence, I had not been prepared to step forward, to put myself on the line, to enter the danger zone. Where was the justice in that?

*Lord,*
*I pray that you will help me to see the needs of the*
  *poor,*
*the marginalized, the homeless, the dispossessed.*
*And help me, I pray, to deny myself and serve them.*

## John 11.35

Jesus began to weep.

Why is there persecution? Why is there no debt relief? Where is the justice? Important questions to ask. Important demands to make. Orphaned as a young child, as important as these questions were, I could not escape the small voice and the questions – why was I all alone? Where is the justice? How easy it was, as I grew up, continually to voice other questions, when all I wanted to ask Jesus was my one, hidden, angry question.

As I grew older the voice became quieter and the question forgotten, at least by me. Then I felt myself asking, 'If I love God, why am I so angry?' The anger was uncorked, the question remembered, fresher and more raw than before. 'Is it fair, Lord, that I was left all alone?' 'No, it was not fair', said the Lord, 'but every night you wept, you did not weep alone as I wept with you'. I then remembered Jesus' sacrifice for me, the lack of justice, the abandonment, the aloneness. Had I wept for him? Had I wept alongside him?

Jesus desires justice, and part of our walk with him is to seek justice for others. But Jesus asks much more – that which is as important and that which we can all do, even when justice is out of reach – not to leave on their own those whose lives are oppressed by injustice, but to come alongside and weep.

*Lord Jesus,*
*help us not to abandon those who seek justice,*
*but to come alongside and weep.*

## Romans 3.22b–25

For there is no distinction, since all have sinned and fall short of the glory of God; they are now justified by his grace as a gift, through the redemption that is in Christ Jesus, whom God put forward as a sacrifice of atonement by his blood, effective through faith.

The chapel was clean and bright and the linen freshly pressed. As candles were lit, expectation was aroused among the small but devout congregation. Those present were not there out of duty; they were there because they wanted to be. They really wanted to celebrate the Eucharist, to remember the Lord's death and resurrection and what it meant for their lives.

Yet this service was different; high walls, physical and electronic searches on entry, bars, gates, cameras and prison officers were all present to remind me that, despite the familiar words and actions, there was something special about this particular service. It took place in Whitemoor, a maximum security prison for men in the top two categories of offender. It's a place in which you don't have to spend too much time for issues of justice to surface.

In a conversation after the service, a prison officer expressed how much she hated being in the chapel. She knew what each of these offenders had done, and yet here they were with forgiveness being freely declared over them: murderers and rapists alike, all washed in the blood of the Lamb. Where's the justice in that?

Yet who are we even to ask that question? We may not have committed the kind of crimes that result in life imprisonment, but not one of us could stand before God without fear of punishment had his loving justice not been met in Christ on our behalf. For it was he that bore God's judgement on our sin.

*Heavenly Father,*
*thank you that your Son came into the world*
*to bring salvation through his death on the cross.*
*Help me, I pray, to avoid condemning others*
*when I am so much in need of forgiveness.*

## Luke 19.1–10

He entered Jericho and was passing through it. A man was there named Zacchaeus; he was a chief tax collector and was rich. He was trying to see who Jesus was, but on account of the crowd he could not, because he was short in stature. So he ran ahead and climbed a sycamore tree to see him, because he was going to pass that way. When Jesus came to the place, he looked up and said to him, 'Zacchaeus, hurry and come down; for I must stay at your house today.' So he hurried down and was happy to welcome him. All who saw it began to grumble and said, 'He has gone to be the guest of one who is a sinner.' Zacchaeus stood there and said to the Lord, 'Look, half of my possessions, Lord, I will give to the poor; and if I have defrauded anyone of anything, I will pay back four times as much.' Then Jesus said to him, 'Today salvation has come to this house, because he too is a son of Abraham. For the Son of Man came to seek out and to save the lost.'

'He's coming, he's coming!' I peer through the leafy branches to where the excited crowd is thronging below. 'He's coming!' Perched precariously on my branch, I see him approaching, surrounded by eager, expectant faces. I'm grateful that they don't notice me in my lofty hiding place.

But then, coming towards the tree, he stops for a moment, looks up at me and says, 'Come down, Zacchaeus. I want to stay at your house today.'

Suddenly all eyes are fixed on me; hostile, resentful eyes. Eyes that carry stories of the money I've swindled, the people I've used for my own gain. Eyes that don't forget. Eyes that demand justice.

But Jesus' eyes too are fixed on me. His eyes see the guilt and shame, the searing pain and embarrassment of the crowd's rejection. He knows that I deserve their anger and scorn, but in his eyes there is only love. Undeserved grace.

And so, still looking at me, he asks again, 'Come down, Zacchaeus.'

And in that moment, looking into Jesus' eyes, I know that I can come down. In the warmth of his gaze I discover a new strength, strength to offer recompense to those that I've wronged, strength to make a new start.

*'I'm coming down, Lord, I'm coming.'*

## John 21.4–7a, 12–19

Just after daybreak, Jesus stood on the beach; but the disciples did not know that it was Jesus. Jesus said to them, 'Children, you have no fish, have you?' They answered him, 'No.' He said to them, 'Cast the net to the right side of the boat, and you will find some.' So they cast it, and now they were not able to haul it in because there were so many fish. That disciple whom Jesus loved said to Peter, 'It is the Lord!'

Jesus said to them, 'Come and have breakfast.' Now none of the disciples dared to ask him, 'Who are you?' because they knew it was the Lord. Jesus came and took the bread and gave it to them, and did the same with the fish. This was now the third time that Jesus appeared to the disciples after he was raised from the dead. When they had finished breakfast, Jesus said to Simon Peter, 'Simon son of John, do you love me more than these?' He said to him, 'Yes, Lord; you know that I love you.' Jesus said to him, 'Feed my lambs.' A second time he said to him, 'Simon son of John, do you love me?' He said to him, 'Yes, Lord; you know that I love you.' Jesus said to him, 'Tend my sheep.' He said to him the third time, 'Simon son of John, do you love me?' Peter felt hurt because he said to him the third time, 'Do you love me?' And he said to him, 'Lord, you know everything; you know that I love you.' Jesus said to him, 'Feed my sheep. Very truly, I tell you, when you were younger, you used to fasten your own belt and to go wherever you wished. But when you grow old, you will stretch out your hands, and someone else will fasten a belt around you and take you where you do not wish to go.' (He said this to indicate the kind of death by which he would glorify God.) After this he said to him, 'Follow me.'

Did Peter desire justice? He offered to follow Jesus to the death. And he denied Jesus three times. What would justice require?

A fruitless night, fishing, so like the night Jesus first called them. Suddenly a stranger points them to fish, more than they can manage. But not a stranger...

Breakfast is cooking on the beach. Jesus invites them to eat. Meals were such an important part of life for Jesus; sometimes with the great or the powerful, often with the outcast or sinner. And now he was eating with his disciples again. And afterwards – questions to Peter, not once, but three times. It seemed so obvious to Peter that he loved Jesus. Yet he had denied him...

And then the call to follow! For Peter there was fresh, unexpected life on the far side of loss and failure. Can this be right?

Easter makes all the difference. On the cross Jesus bears the consequence of wrongdoing. It is not ignored, not pushed under the carpet, but dealt with. His resurrection is the first fruits of God's new creation, remade through the cross.

Peter receives this unexpected, Easter justice; he is completely forgiven. In a similar way, the Lord's Prayer calls on us to forgive those who have hurt or failed us, to be reconciled as we look forward to worshipping God together in the kingdom that Jesus brings.

*Lord God,*
*you called Peter to care for your church*
*even though he had betrayed you.*
*Forgive me for my sins, I pray,*
*and strengthen me to forgive those who hurt me.*

# The Contributors

Sarah Aebersold, Sam Brazier, Rob Crofton, Ben Dean, Linda Duckers, Kit Gunasekera, Anthony Hammill, Mary Hancock, James Heard, Richard Higginson, Philip Hobday, Craig Holmes, Lisa Jackson, Rachel Jenkinson, Philip Jenson, Alastair Kirk, Sarah Lawrence, Sam Leach, Hayley Matthews, Peter Mayo-Smith, Rob McDonald, Nicholas McKee, Ash Meaney, Ian Pallent, Eve Pegler, Marcus Pickering, Ingrid Randall, Jon Randall, Diana Rees-Jones, Oliver Ryder, Margaret Shropshire, Brian Streeter, Hannah Sutcliffe, Trevor Thorn, Catherine Vaughan, Mike Volland, Jon Ward, Richard Wilson, Susan Wilson, Naomi Wormell

# About Ridley Hall

Ridley Hall is an Anglican Theological College which is celebrating its 125th anniversary as this book is being published. It is a member of the Cambridge Theological Federation. There is a great deal going on at Ridley Hall: the formation of men and women for ordained ministry; the training of youth pastors and workers; the supporting of business people in their working lives; the continuing ministerial education of Lay Readers and licensed Lay Ministers, a sabbatical programme – and much more! We are here to serve God's people and prepare God's people for the challenges and opportunities that the twenty-first century presents to the Church.

All development work at Ridley Hall depends on voluntary gifts. If you have found this book helpful and would like to support the work of the College further, a donation would be greatly appreciated at The Development Office, Ridley Hall, Cambridge, CB3 9HG. The Development Officer would also be very pleased to hear from anyone who might consider leaving a legacy in favour of the College, thus helping to ensure that leaders for the Church of the twenty-first century will continue to be trained to the highest standards possible. Telephone +44 (0)1223 741069 (direct line). Ridley Hall is a registered charity: no. 311456.

Ridley Hall is home to Grove Books, publishers of 28-page explorations of Christian life and ministry, covering a wide range of topics, from fair trade to forgiveness and from mission strategy to marriage. Booklets cost just £2.95 each, and are written by practitioners, not theorists, in eight series: Biblical, Ethics, Evangelism, Pastoral, Renewal, Spirituality, Worship and Youth.

Call 01223 464748 for a stocklist or visit the Grove website at www.grovebooks.co.uk.

# Other Opportunities at Ridley Hall

Resource & Refresh (R&R) is a rolling programme of short residential events in April and September each year, primarily for resourcing and refreshing Church of England Licensed Readers / Licensed Lay Ministers. If, as a Reader or Licensed Lay Minister, you long to be inspired and stretched in your faith, these are events for YOU. Drawing on the imagination and expertise of Ridley Hall, the Cambridge (multi-denominational) Theological Federation, University links and the wider region, R&R promises to spur Readers and Licensed Lay Ministers on in their ministry – intellectually, practically and spiritually. For further information and to see endorsements of some who have attended earlier courses, write to The Administrator, Reader R&R, Ridley Hall, Cambridge, CB3 9HG or visit our website at www.ridley.cam.ac.uk following the specific 'Readers' Courses' link in the drop-down 'Courses' menu. While these courses are primarily designed for Anglican lay Readers, most would be appropriate for lay teachers and preachers of other denominations who would be very welcome, but they would need to recognize the worship pattern on the courses will be Anglican in its nature. If you would like to discuss the appropriateness of any particular course for people of other denominations, call Trevor Thorn on 01223 741069 or email tt219@cam.ac.uk.

Ridley Hall also welcomes independent (self financing) full- and part-time students to study alongside those training for ordination and youth ministry. It is possible to start a one-, two- or three-year course each September, studying to certificate, diploma or degree level. In 2006–07 we expect to be launching a new one-year Certificate in Mission and Evangelism. Further information can be found on the College website – www.ridley.cam.ac.uk – or obtained from the PA to the Principal at Ridley Hall, Cambridge, CB3 9HG.